EARTHQUAKES FOR SMARTYPANTS

Anushka Ravishankar
Illustrations by Pia Alizé Hazarika

duckbill

An imprint of Penguin Random House

DUCKBILL BOOKS

USA | Canada | UK | Ireland | Australia
New Zealand | India | South Africa | China | Singapore

Duckbill Books is part of the Penguin Random House group of companies
whose addresses can be found at global.penguinrandomhouse.com

Published by Penguin Random House India Pvt. Ltd
4th Floor, Capital Tower 1, MG Road,
Gurugram 122 002, Haryana, India

Penguin
Random House
India

First published in Duckbill Books by
Penguin Random House India 2023

Text copyright © Anushka Ravishankar 2023
Illustrations copyright © Pia Alizé Hazarika 2023

ISBN 9780143461012

Typeset in ArcherPro by DiTech Publishing Services Pvt. Ltd
Printed at Thomson Press India Ltd, New Delhi

www.penguin.co.in

An **EARTHQUAKE** is the sudden release of
energy in the Earth's crust, resulting in waves of
shaking, or seismic waves, that radiate outwards from

When the surface of the Earth shakes, it is called an **earthquake**. It happens when the **crust** of the Earth moves.

I KNOW YOU LIKE IT, BUT YOU CAN'T EAT THIS CRUST.
BECAUSE IT'S NOT BREAD!

The Earth's **crust** is the surface or the top layer of the Earth. The crust, along with the hard layer below it, form the **lithosphere**.

CRUST

MANTLE
OUTER CORE
INNER CORE

LITHOSPHERE

The lithosphere is made up of **plates**.

These plates are called **tectonic plates.**
They are actually HUGE blocks of rock!

I WON'T CALL THEM ROCKS.
OR ROCKY PLATES.
BECAUSE TECTONIC PLATES IS THE NAME GIVEN TO THEM.

Under the lithosphere is a softer
layer called the **asthenosphere**.

It's a gooey, plasticky kind
of layer.

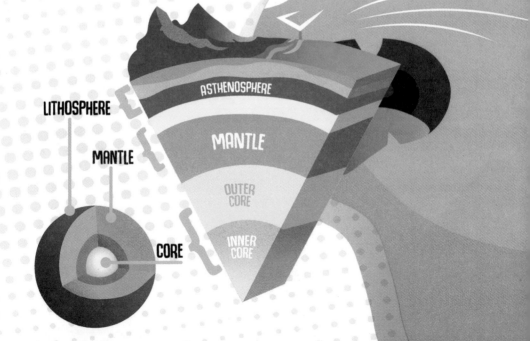

THE INSIDE OF THE EARTH LOOKS A BIT LIKE A RAINBOW CAKE, YES.
NO, YOU CAN'T EAT IT.
WHY? THIS IS THE EARTH! IT'S BIG!
NO, I'M NOT GETTING YOU CAKE.

CRUST

LITHOSPHERE

ASTHENOSPHERE

The tectonic plates slide very slowly over the asthenosphere. Sometimes they slide towards each other and sometimes they slide apart.

NO, NOT THAT KIND OF SLIDE.
NO, THEY DON'T GO TO A PARK!
AND THEY DON'T HAVE FUN.
BECAUSE THE SLIDING HAPPENS REALLY SLOWLY.

Any push or pull that makes an object move is called a **force**.

There are many forces deep in the Earth, like heat and gravity*. These are always pushing and pulling the plates and trying to make them move.

These are called **tectonic forces**.

(*Gravity for Smartypants)

OKAY, OKAY, YOU'RE A TECTONIC FORCE.
JUST DON'T BREAK THOSE PLATES, PLEASE!

When the plates move, sometimes a break forms in the Earth's crust. These breaks are called **fault lines**.

The plates can move in many different directions.

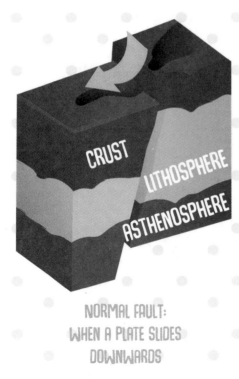

CRUST

LITHOSPHERE

ASTHENOSPHERE

CRUST

LITHOSPHERE

ASTHENOSPHERE

NORMAL FAULT:
WHEN A PLATE SLIDES
DOWNWARDS

REVERSE FAULT:
WHEN A PLATE SLIDES
UPWARDS

THAT IS DEFINITELY YOUR FAULT, BUT WE'RE TALKING ABOUT A DIFFERENT KIND OF FAULT.
not my fault
CRUST
LITHOSPHERE
ASTHENOSPHERE
STRIKE SLIP FAULT: WHEN TWO PLATES SLIDE PAST EACH OTHE

The plates, sometimes, get stuck against each other and stop moving. But they are still being pushed and pulled against each other along the fault lines by the tectonic forces.

Most earthquakes happen because of the fault lines.

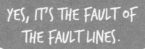

Sometimes, the plates are pushed so hard that the rocks suddenly come unstuck! When that happens, a lot of force is let out.

It's a bit like a tug-of-war. When both sides are pulling equally hard, the rope stays still, or moves only slowly. Suppose, suddenly, a strong person joins one side and gives a really hard tug . . .

YES, SOMEONE STRONG LIKE YOU.
YES, YOU COULD DO IT ALL BY YOURSELF.
OKAY, BUT WHAT WOULD HAPPEN?

BOOM!

Everyone falls down because of the sudden force that is let out.

In an earthquake, when the plates move suddenly, the force that is let out is so strong, it is hard to imagine!

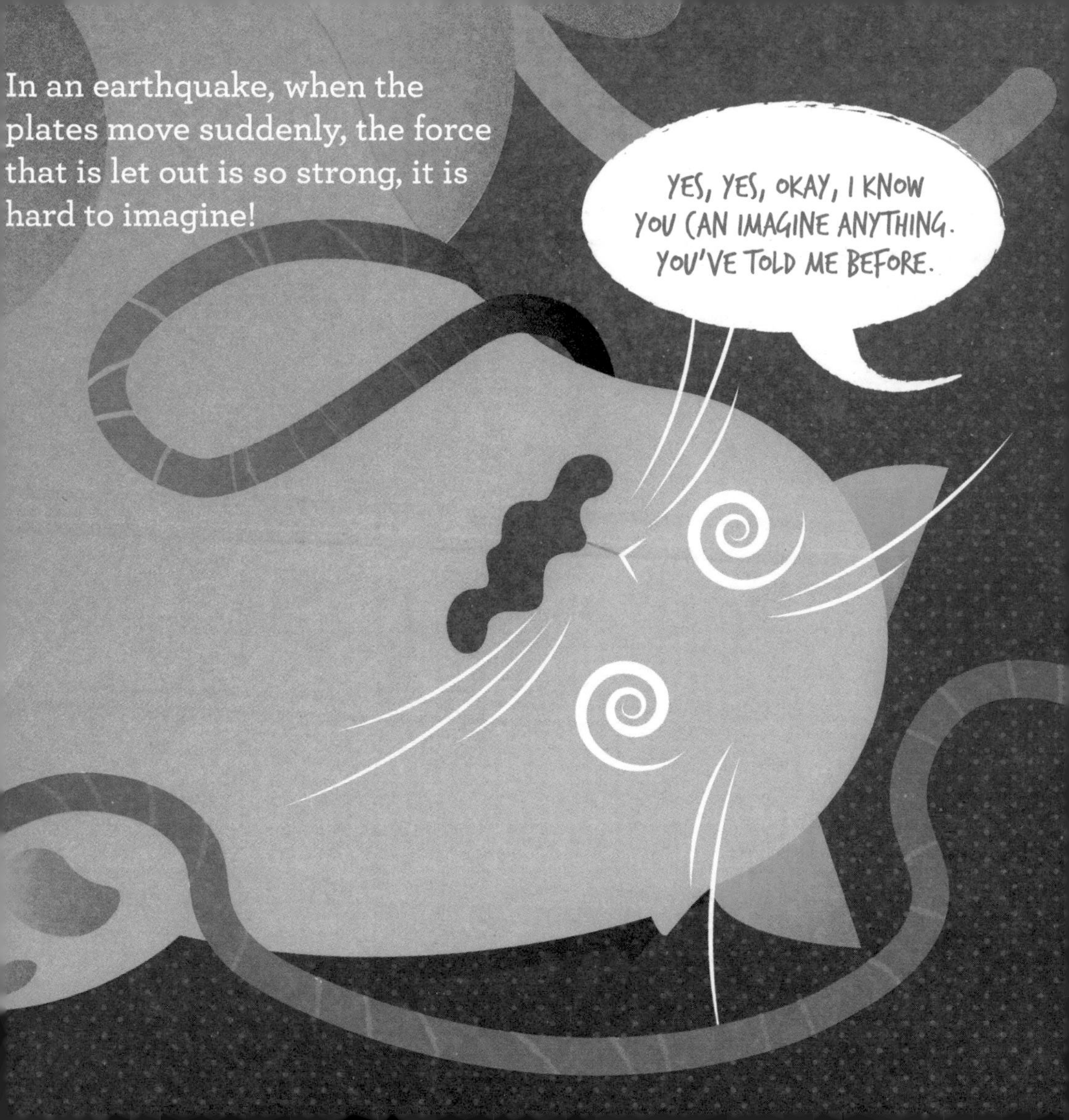

Imagine throwing a stone in a lake.

Bloop!

You would be able to see the ripples in the water. The force in an earthquake moves through the layers of the Earth like those ripples move in the water. These movements are called **seismic waves**.

NO, YOU CAN'T HIT A FISH.
NO, YOU CAN'T SEE THE FISH. THIS LAKE HAS NO FISH.

The point at which ripples start is called the focus of the earthquake. It's like the place where the stone hits the water. The **epicenter** is the point on the surface of the Earth, which is just above the focus.

Some of these waves move inside the Earth, travelling through solids and liquids in the inner layers of the Earth.

These are body waves.

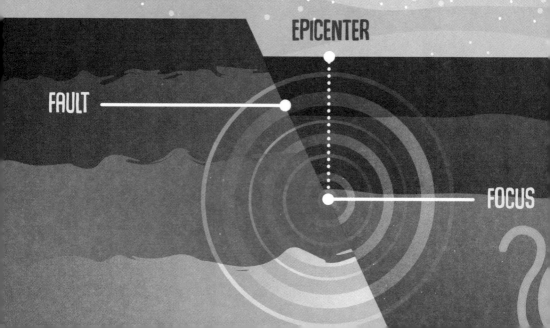

EPICENTER

FAULT

FOCUS

AARGH. NOT THAT KIND OF BODY WAVE!
BECAUSE THEY ARE WAVES, NOT DANCERS.

Then there are the **surface waves** that move along the surface of the Earth, destroying everything in the way.

The surface waves move much slower than the body waves. That's why it's only at the end of the earthquake that the surface of the Earth shakes and destruction happens.

THAT WON'T HELP IF THERE'S A BIG EARTHQUAKE.
IF THERE'S A SMALL ONE, YOU'LL JUST FEEL THINGS SHAKING A LITTLE.

One earthquake can cause other plates to move along other fault lines, leading to more earthquakes. The biggest earthquake is called the **mainshock**. The smaller ones that happen before and after that are called **foreshocks** and **aftershocks**.

These shocks or earthquakes are also called **tremors**.

NO, THEY ARE NOT ELECTRIC SHOCKS, SO WEARING RUBBER SHOES WON'T HELP.

The **magnitude** or size of the earthquake is a number that tells you how big the earthquake is.

Just as your weight is measured by how much you weigh on a weighing scale, the size of an earthquake is measured by how much it measures on the Richter scale.

1.0
MICRO

2.0–3.0
MINOR

4.0
LIGHT

5.0
MODERATE

NO, AN EARTHQUAKE CANNOT STAND ON A RICHTER SCALE.
YES, I KNOW YOU CAN STAND ON THE WEIGHING SCALE. GOOD FOR YOU.
6.0 STRONG
7.0 MAJOR
8.0 - 10.0 SEVERE

A seismograph is used to measure the strength of an earthquake.

An earthquake that is less than three on the Richter scale cannot even be felt by humans. If it is over seven on the Richter scale, it is considered a major earthquake.

NO, THERE'S NO EARTHQUAKE NOW.

I KNOW BECAUSE IF THERE WAS ONE, IT WOULD HAVE BEEN ON THE NEWS.

THEY HAVE WAYS OF KNOWING.

OKAY, STOP. I KNOW THAT'S YOU MOVING MY CHAIR.
YES, THAT'S HOW IT WOULD MOVE IN AN EARTHQUAKE.
YES, YOU KNOW ALL ABOUT EARTHQUAKES NOW, SMARTYPANTS.

Anushka Ravishankar likes science, cats and books, not necessarily in that order. So she decided to write a book to explain science to a cat. The cat doesn't always get the point, but she hopes her readers will.

Pia Alizé Hazarika is an illustrator primarily interested in comics and visual narratives.

Her independent/collaborative work has been published by Penguin Random House India (*The PAO Anthology*), Comix India, Manta Ray Comics, The Pulpocracy, Captain Bijli Comics, Yoda Press, Zubaan Books and the Khoj Artists Collective. She runs PIG Studio, an illustration-driven space, based out of New Delhi.

Her handle on Instagram is @_PigStudio_